Death Valley National Park

Nate Frisch

Published by
CREATIVE EDUCATION

P.O. Box 227, Mankato, Minnesota 56002
Creative Education is an imprint of The Creative Company
www.thecreativecompany.us

Design and production by Danny Nanos of Gilbert & Nanos
Art direction by Rita Marshall
Printed in the United States of America

Photographs by Alamy (North Wind Picture Archives, Photoshot Holdings Ltd.), Getty Images (Antenna Audio Inc., Kick Images, Richard Nebesky), Shutterstock (Antonio Abrignani, agap, Galyna Andrushko, Jeff Banke, Katrina Brown, Bufo, George Burba, ChipPix, Cusan, Rusty Dodson, julius fekete, Jim Feliciano, Don Fink, Jorg Hackemann, Michael Hare, Candace Hartley, iofoto, Mariusz S. Jurgielewicz, Anne Kitzman, Keith LeBlanc, Doug Lemke, Lukich, Manamana, Rodney Mehring, Jason Mintzer, KellyNelson, pashabo, Dean Pennala, pixy, Bev Ram, Elena Ray, rook76, Jason Patrick Ross, Sally Scott, Joel Shawn, SipaPhoto, Nelson Sirlin, Nickolay Stanev, Ultrashock, david vadala, robert paul van beets, Cedric Weber, Brian Weed, worldwildlifewonders, Andrey Yurlov, Ziablik)

Library of Congress Cataloging-in-Publication Data

Frisch, Nate.
Death Valley National Park / by Nate Frisch.
p. cm. — (Preserving America)
Includes bibliographical references and index.
Summary: An exploration of Death Valley National Park, including how its desert landscape was formed, its history
of preservation, and tourist attractions such as the historic mansion called Scotty's Castle.
ISBN 978-1-60818-194-0
1. Death Valley National Park (Calif. and Nev.)—Juvenile literature. I. Title.
F868.D2F75 2013
979.4'87—dc23   2012023228

FIRST EDITION

2 4 6 8 9 7 5 3 1

Cover & page 3: *Sand dunes near Stovepipe Wells; a black widow spider*

CREATIVE EDUCATION

Death Valley National Park

Nate Frisch

Table of Contents

TOWERING MOUNTAINS and glassy lakes. Churning rivers and dense forests. Lush prairies and baking deserts. The open spaces and natural wonders of the United States once seemed as limitless as they were diverse. But as human expansion and development increased in the 1800s, forests and prairies were replaced by settlements and agricultural lands. Waterways were diverted, wildlife was over-hunted, and the earth was scarred by mining. Fortunately, many Americans fought to preserve some of the country's vanishing wilderness. In 1872, Yellowstone National Park was established, becoming the first true national park in the world and paving the way for future preservation efforts. In 1901, Theodore Roosevelt became U.S. president. He once stated, "There can be no greater issue than that of conservation in this country," and during his presidency, Roosevelt signed five national parks into existence. The National Park Service (NPS) was created in 1916 to manage the growing number of U.S. parks. In 1994, Death Valley National Park was established in California and Nevada. Featuring a surprising diversity of life, as well as a compelling history of human habitation, this scorching desert preserve has prevailed over a deadly reputation to become one of America's most distinctive and intriguing parks.

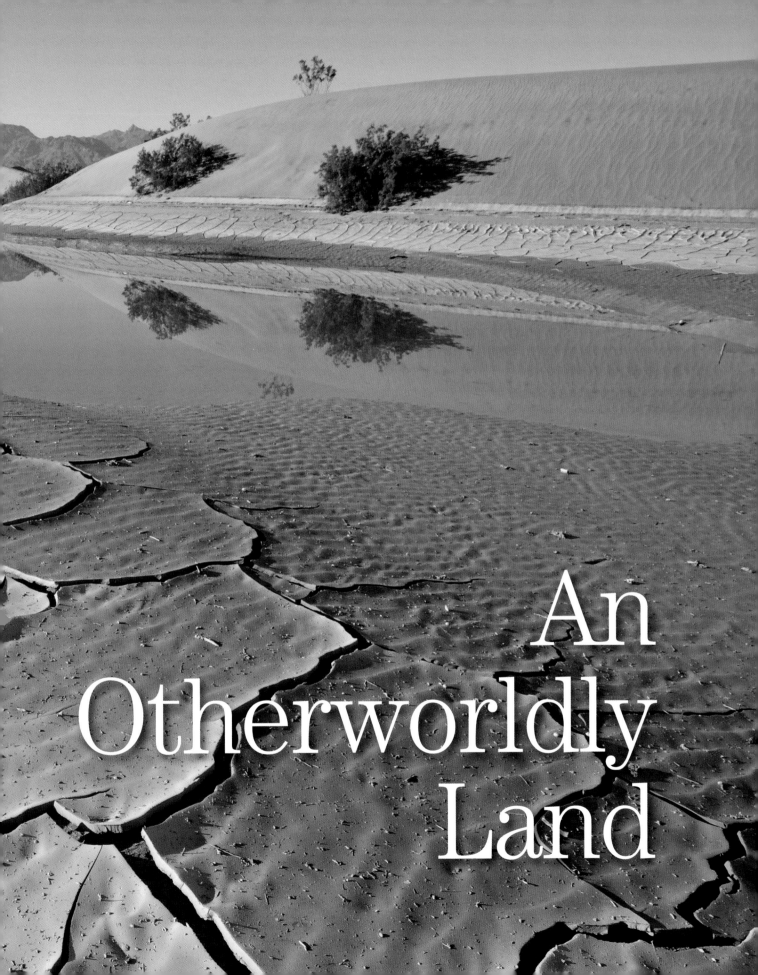

An Otherworldly Land

Death Valley is a region of extremes to which the phrase "hottest, driest, lowest" is often applied. A temperature of 134 °F (57 °C) was recorded there in 1913, and that remains the hottest official temperature ever recorded in the Western Hemisphere. The valley floor of Death Valley averages just 2 inches (5 cm) of precipitation per year, while the potential evaporation rate is 150 inches (381 cm) per year. Death Valley's lowest point—in Badwater Basin—is 282 feet (85.5 m) below sea level, making it the lowest point in North America.

While these extremes are remarkable, the combination of geological factors that created this parched, otherworldly region is equally unique. Death Valley is located in the northwestern corner of the Mojave Desert, which is situated in the western portion of the Great Basin region. Many millions of years ago, the region featured tropical forests and shallow seas, and as little as about 20,000 years ago during **ice ages**, large lakes were present.

Aside from global climate change, Death Valley's transformation into a desert was largely caused by the formation of the Sierra Nevada mountain range just west of the region. About 25 million years ago, an enormous chunk of Earth's crust broke loose near what is now eastern California. This section of earth began to tilt, and its eastern edge continually rose for millions of years, reaching heights of more than 14,000 feet (4,267 m). The high elevation of this mountain range, which runs generally north and south, created a large rain shadow to the east where the Mojave Desert now lies.

Badwater Basin is so named because the basin has a small pool of spring-fed water that is salty and therefore bad, or undrinkable

A rain shadow is caused when air or weather systems (which typically move from west to east) meet mountains. For the air to continue eastward, it must rise to clear the land. As the air rises, the colder temperatures of the higher elevations cause moisture in the air to condense and fall as rain or snow. By the time the weather system passes over the mountains, it has lost all or nearly all of its moisture, and the land for many miles beyond the mountains will be almost completely lacking in precipitation and humidity. Death Valley is at the western edge of the rain shadow created by the Sierra Nevadas, and in between that moisture-blocking wall and Death Valley's lowlands are the Panamint Mountains, which further wring out what little moisture may sneak past the Sierra Nevadas.

Although usually short-lived, shallow water pools can add to Death Valley's beauty; this pool reflects the Panamint Mountains

The resulting absence of precipitation and humidity in the air has a broad and constant impact on Death Valley. Air without moisture changes temperatures rapidly according to the presence or absence of the sun. This explains, in part, why daytime summer temperatures in Death Valley frequently surpass 120 °F (49 °C) and why nighttime summer lows are often more than 30 °F (17 °C) colder. Another factor in Death Valley's climate is the region's southerly location in the U.S. But what separates Death Valley from other desert regions in the Great Basin and makes it one of the hottest places in the world is its elevation.

Temperatures anywhere in the world vary at different elevations due to differing amounts of air pressure. Lower elevations have more air pressure and tend to be warmer than higher elevations. Typically, temperature changes at an increase of 3 to 5 °F (2 to 3 °C) for every 1,000 feet (305 m) of drop in elevation. Death Valley's low point of 282 feet (85.5 m) below sea level in Badwater Basin is about 3,000 feet (914 m) below the average elevation of the Mojave Desert, meaning temperatures will often be 9 to 15 °F (6 to 8 °C) hotter in Badwater than in the surrounding desert. Meanwhile, Death Valley's highest point—Telescope Peak, at 11,049 feet (3,368 m)—will be significantly cooler.

While discussions of Death Valley often begin and end with its extremes, the region contains more diverse landforms than is often imagined. The main valley for which the region is named is a graben—a sunken area of Earth's crust between two **faults**. This graben is up to 15 miles (24 km) wide, walled in on either side by the Panamint Mountains to the west and the Amargosa Mountains to the east. Even within Death Valley are many smaller mountains and canyons. Because of the area's wide range of altitudes, Death Valley features snow-capped mountains as well as wind-blown sand dunes and sunbaked salt flats.

The formation of sand dunes—such as Death Valley's Mesquite Flat dunes—requires a combination of loose sand, wind, and a place for sand to collect. The loose sand needed comes from **eroded** canyons and **washes**. Death Valley tends to be windy most of the time, which contributes both to erosion and the relocation of sand. Often the wind simultaneously picks up and drops sand as it moves across the landscape and therefore disperses the sediment more or less evenly. But if the wind is blocked by mountains or some other barrier, it drops sand without picking any up. As the trapped sand and wind swirl, expanses of sand hills or dunes are formed.

Death Valley's salt flats (pictured) and other level, barren terrain make for great running grounds for the fleet-footed roadrunner

Salt flats are indeed salty but not always flat. Despite Death Valley's **arid** climate, occasional rain or melting snow from higher elevations sometimes drains to lower ground, dissolving and carrying minerals from the mountain slopes along the way. This mineral-rich water collects in Death Valley's deep basins. A water pool as wide as a small lake may completely dry up in a matter of days, but left behind are salt and various other minerals that form crystals. Over thousands of years, layers of these crystals build up, forming a brittle crust on the ground. More common than sand dunes, salt flats cover about 200 square miles (518 sq km) of Death Valley, including Badwater. Salt flats that are free of dust or sand can appear blindingly white under intense sunlight. Death Valley also features large playas, or dry lakebeds. These are similar to salt flats in some ways but lack the layers of mineral buildup.

While many of Death Valley's mountains, dunes, flats, and otherwise rugged terrain seem inhospitable to life, a surprising number of hardy plant and animal species inhabit the region. With its up-and-down landscape, Death Valley features 10 distinct vegetation zones, and the region's more than 1,000 plant species range from various cacti to pine trees to wildflowers. Cacti can be found at most elevations year round, while trees grow mostly in higher woodlands. Death Valley sometimes sprouts seemingly miraculous, sprawling fields of wildflowers, but such events occur only under ideal conditions. The vast majority of the year, wildflowers exist as seeds in the ground, drawn out only by rare rain showers that must be gentle enough to not wash the seeds away yet substantial enough to soak the soil. How long the resulting flowers live further depends on rain, wind, and heat.

Animals, too, may be constant fixtures in the Death Valley region, or they may come and go, depending on conditions. All told, 51 native mammal species, 307 birds, 36 reptiles, 3 amphibians, and 5 fish have been identified within Death Valley. The largest creatures—most of which live at higher elevations—include bighorn sheep, mule deer, mountain lions, coyotes, and bobcats, but these are far outnumbered by smaller animals, such as the nearly 20 species of mice and rats. The region's diverse reptile species include desert tortoises, horned lizards, and rattlesnakes. Among birds, roadrunners are iconic, year-round residents, and several species of pupfish are unique to Death Valley's few spring-fed pools or streams.

Death Valley's bighorn sheep are called desert bighorns and are generally smaller than bighorns found in mountains farther north

Overcoming A Bad Rap

It is one thing to imagine animals adapting to the harsh climate and unforgiving landscape of Death Valley. It is another to comprehend humans voluntarily living there. Yet the region has a nearly 10,000-year history of human habitation. The first inhabitants, known as the Nevares Spring People, experienced a milder climate, as the land was still being affected by an ice age when they resided there. These people were hunter-gatherers who benefited from the presence of more numerous large animals and readily available water. Over the next several thousand years, other groups appeared in the region. Conditions grew steadily harsher, but the people's methods and tools for hunting and gathering also advanced, allowing them to survive in this bleak land.

About 1,000 years ago, the Timbisha Shoshone Indians arrived in Death Valley. They moved up and down in elevation in accordance with the seasons, which made temperatures more tolerable and kept the natives in proximity to the plants and animals upon which they depended. Plant food sources such as pinyon pine nuts were collected at high elevations in the fall, and mesquite beans were collected at low elevations in the spring. This ongoing cycle of vertical migration continued for centuries before the first European-Americans entered the valley.

This stamp depicts Sutter's Mill and commemorates the California Gold Rush—an event that helped change the American West

In 1848, gold was found at a sawmill called Sutter's Mill about 300 miles (483 km) northwest of Death Valley. When news got out, the California Gold Rush began. One group of gold seekers set out in 120 wagons from Salt Lake City, Utah, in October 1849, intent on reaching California. These "49ers" decided to follow a trade route called the Old Spanish Trail

around the southern end of the Sierra Nevadas rather than risk going over the mountains so close to winter. Just a few years earlier, the mountains had claimed the lives of nearly half of the now famous Donner Party.

The prospectors found the Old Spanish Trail safe, but the pace was slow, and its roundabout route made many of the travelers impatient. About 20 oxen-pulled wagons split off from the main group for what was supposed to be a shortcut. The decision quickly proved reckless. First, the travelers encountered a difficult crossing at Beaver Dam Wash, a canyon near the Utah–Nevada border. Then they struggled westward through the desert for more than a month, almost dying of thirst. They reached Death Valley in late December, which was fortuitous, since temperatures during this winter period were relatively mild and water was more plentiful. Still, both humans and oxen were weary from the two months of travel and limited food. These problems were compounded as the 49ers wandered the valley for weeks in an unsuccessful search for paths leading over or through the many mountains.

In the mid-1800s, California came to be seen as a land of opportunity, though most gold prospectors never actually struck it rich

Unable to find a clear path for the wagons to follow out of the valley, the travelers decided they would have to exit on foot. They butchered their oxen and burned their wagons to cook the meat at a site that is still referred to as Burned Wagons Camp. With fuller bellies and unencumbered by wagons, the party finally made its way out of the valley. Supposedly, as the group took a final look back, one of the pioneers said, "Goodbye, Death Valley," and the region has been known by that name ever since. In fact, although the conditions were brutal and dangerous, only one elderly member of the party died in the desert valley.

Despite the ominous name, some prospectors soon deliberately went to Death Valley in search of gold, and during the 1850s, gold and silver mining were common in the region. This slowed as the Gold Rush craze died down, but Death Valley saw a resurgence of mining in the late 1800s and early 1900s, and discoveries of gold, silver, copper, and lead spurred the development of **boom towns**. As an area ran out of ore, though, such settlements were quickly deserted, becoming ghost towns. Rhyolite, the largest such city near Death Valley, once had a population of several thousand people (its ruins can today be seen just east of the current national park boundaries).

Ghost towns are especially common in deserts, as there is often little to keep people there except the possibility of mineral riches

While efforts to find precious metals in Death Valley were hit-and-miss, a steadier kind of mining began in the late 1800s—the extraction of borax. Borax is a mineral that was often used in soap and various home remedies at the time, and it was useful for other industrial purposes as well. In 1881, William T. Coleman, a California businessman, filed huge mining **claims** to obtain land in Death Valley and later established the Harmony Borax Works company in the valley near Furnace Creek.

Because of Death Valley's remote location, getting the mined borax to the nearest railroad—whose tracks were 165 miles (265 km) away on

the other side of the Panamint Mountains—was a major obstacle. The problem was solved with an innovative solution: the creation of 20-mule teams to pull massive wagonloads of the ore from Death Valley southwest to the town of Mojave. The teams often had 18 mules and 2 horses, and they generally pulled 2 full wagons of borax plus a water tank, which made for a total weight of more than 35 tons (32 t). The round-trip journey took 20 days, and the operation went year round, even in temperatures above 120 °F (49 °C). This method of transportation went on from 1883 to 1889, and not only was it an effective hauling method, it was also its own advertising ploy. The 20-mule teams became an enduring symbol of borax, even after Harmony Borax Works was bought out and became the Pacific Coast Borax Company in 1890 and expanded railways made the mule teams obsolete.

While borax mining continued, the first signs of tourism in Death Valley emerged in the 1920s, when tent-like structures near present-day

Mules are strong, hardy, and intelligent pack animals, and they have long played roles in Death Valley prospecting and mining

The water tank was a heavy but critical component of the mule-drawn, borax-loaded wagons that became a Death Valley icon

Stovepipe Wells represented the first resort accommodations. Later, the Pacific Coast Borax Company converted the Furnace Creek Ranch—which had been housing workers of the borax operations—into Furnace Creek Inn & Resort. Natural springs were a big draw for tourists, many of whom believed the waters had curative properties. To capitalize on this, Furnace Creek Inn & Resort management diverted water from nearby springs to create larger, more impressive pools.

In 1922, construction began on a building that came to be known as Scotty's Castle. Situated at Death Valley Ranch, the building was a Mediterranean-style mansion that a prospector named Walter Scott claimed to have built with profits from his secret gold mine. In truth, it was the home of Chicago millionaire Albert Johnson, and Scott had no gold mine at all. Nonetheless, the ruse helped to publicize the building and the region, and Johnson went along with it, eventually turning the home into a resort to capitalize on its popularity.

The increased tourism coincided with a revival of mining interest, and newer machines and methods gouged the earth deeper and faster than ever before. Surprisingly, some of the first suggestions to protect the land came from the Pacific Coast Borax Company. The company's concerns weren't based purely on conservation, though. To the borax company, Death Valley had become more profitable as a tourist destination than as a mining operation, and company officials realized that a region full of mining pits and machines would not appeal to tourists.

In 1926, the company began using magazine and newspaper articles and a radio program called *Death Valley Days* to win public support for the establishment of a national park.

In order for Death Valley to become a national park, the U.S. Congress would need to give its approval, but legislators were torn, with some recognizing Death Valley's worth as a potential park and others focusing on its value to the mining industry. While Congress debated the park's merits, U.S. president Herbert Hoover used his authority to give the region the lesser status of a national monument on February 11, 1933, shortly before his presidential term ended. A long 61 years would pass before Death Valley National Monument would finally become a national park.

Scotty's Castle today draws about 100,000 visitors a year, and tours are led by park rangers dressed in the styles of the 1930s

Uncertain
Conservation

The lengthy interval between Death Valley's inception as a national monument and its designation as a national park left room for many changes and conflicts to take place in the region over the better part of a century. President Hoover's decision to make Death Valley a national monument was largely in reaction to the ways in which mining was altering the landscape, and the designation resulted in mining being banned in the area. However, later in 1933, Congress passed a law that reopened the region to mining. The U.S. was in the midst of the Great Depression—a time when many people had no jobs and little money. The decision to re-allow mining in Death Valley provided work for people not only in the immediate area but also at plants and factories where borax and other ores were refined and made into products. And so, economically helpful but environmentally destructive practices such as open-pit and strip mining continued to reshape Death Valley. Open-pit mining consisted of digging ever deepening and widening pits or holes in the earth in search of ores. In strip mining, huge machines scraped away thick surface layers of the earth across vast areas of land.

Death Valley was subjected to all forms of mining, including open-pit mining, strip mining, and underground mining (pictured)

The Great Depression affected Death Valley in other ways, too. As a response to the high unemployment rate among unskilled laborers, government programs such as the Civilian Conservation Corps (CCC) were formed. The CCC hired young, single men and put them to work building and maintaining roads, bridges, and various other structures on public or government land. These workers also were responsible for maintaining or improving the natural state of these places by planting trees and managing erosion, guarding against forest fires, and monitoring water quality. In Death Valley, the CCC was involved in the construction of 500 miles (805 km) of roadway, nearly 80 buildings, and several campgrounds and picnic areas. The program's workers also installed

telephone lines, assembled water pipes, groomed hiking trails, and even built an airplane landing strip.

In 1938, the CCC was involved in a settlement with the Timbisha Shoshone Indians, who had lived in Death Valley for about 1,000 years. At the time of the creation of Death Valley National Monument, nothing had been laid out concerning the future of the tribe. When the American Indians refused relocation plans set forth by the U.S. government, the NPS agreed to set aside 40 acres (16 ha) of land for the tribe in the heart of Death Valley near Furnace Creek. On that site, the CCC and Timbisha Shoshone built a settlement with **adobe** homes and a trading post. The small village is still occupied by Indians today.

After World War II (1939–45) helped bring an end to the Great Depression, mining for borax and **talc** continued in Death Valley, and with each passing year, the land became more scarred, and mining operations crept closer to tourist centers at Furnace Creek and Stovepipe Wells. Unfortunately, the interest in natural conservation that had peaked in the early 1900s had seemed to die down in the decades that followed (only one national park was established between 1939 and 1961). It wasn't until the late 1960s and early '70s that the conservationist movement experienced a revival, and in 1976, the U.S. Congress passed

The CCC helped to make Death Valley a welcoming destination for visitors with the construction of trails, some close to borax mine ruins (below)

the Mining in Parks Act. This law prevented any new mining claims from being made in Death Valley, and it authorized NPS officials to investigate whether current mining claims were valid or if people had made them just to take ownership of land. Valid mining operations were allowed to continue working on their claims, but certain methods, including pit mining, were banned.

Owing to the stricter regulations and the fact that resources on existing claims began to run out, mining in Death Valley dwindled; the last mining operation, Billie Mine, would close in 2005. Still, evidence of past mining is easily seen in Death Valley today, whether in the form of the 400-foot-deep (122 m) Boraxo Mine, the numerous narrow tunnels leading underground, or earth churned up by strip mining.

As Death Valley's 140 years of mining were winding down, the region finally became a national park on October 31, 1994. It did so as part of the Desert Protection Act, which also established nearby Joshua Tree National Park and the Mojave National Preserve at the same time. For seven years, California senator Dianne Feinstein had led a lobbying effort for the increased protection of these areas, citing their scenic, cultural, ecological, scientific, and recreational value. The establishment of Death Valley National Park brought tighter restrictions to the area, expanded guest

The borax from Death Valley pit mines has been used in such varied products as soap, teeth whiteners, glass, and fertilizers

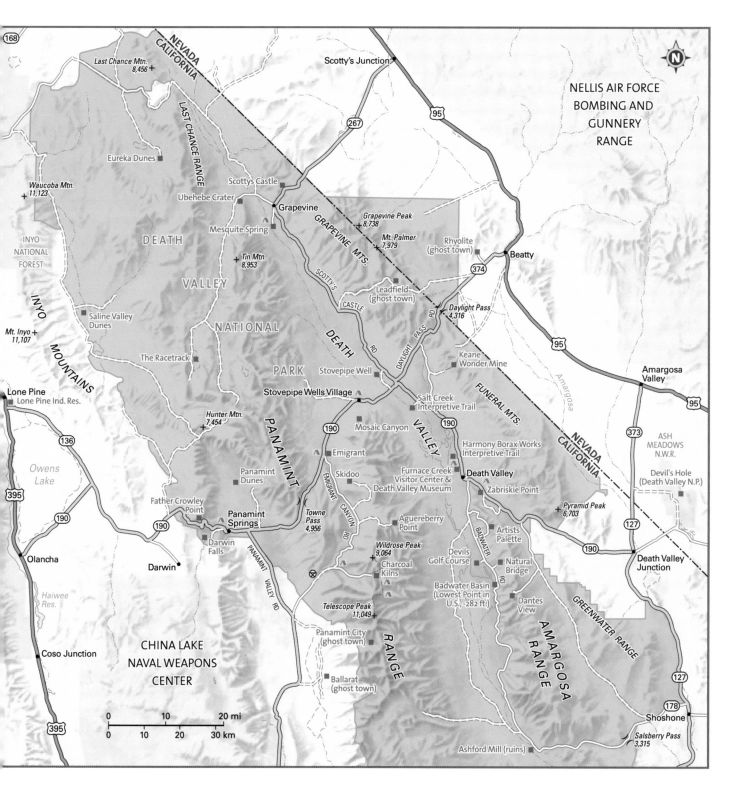

168

NEVADA
CALIFORNIA

Last Chance Mtn.
8,456 +

Scotty's Junction

NELLIS AIR FORCE
BOMBING AND
GUNNERY
RANGE

267

95

Eureka Dunes

LAST CHANCE RANGE

Waucoba Mtn.
+ 11,123

Scottys Castle

Ubehebe Crater

Grapevine

Grapevine Peak
8,738 +

GRAPEVINE MTS.

DEATH

Mesquite Spring

Tin Mtn.
+ 8,953

Mt. Palmer
7,979

Rhyolite
(ghost town)

Beatty

374

INYO
NATIONAL
FOREST

VALLEY

SCOTTY'S

Leadfield
(ghost town)

Daylight Pass
4,316

Saline Valley
Dunes

NATIONAL

CASTLE

DEATH

DAYLIGHT PASS

95

Mt. Inyo +
11,107

RD.

Amargosa

The Racetrack

PARK

Stovepipe Well

Keane
Wonder Mine

Amargosa
Valley

INYO

FUNERAL MTS.

373

NEVADA
CALIFORNIA

ASH
MEADOWS
N.W.R.

Stovepipe Wells Village

Salt Creek
Interpretive Trail

VALLEY

MOUNTAINS

Lone Pine
Lone Pine Ind. Res.

Hunter Mtn.
7,454

190

Mosaic Canyon

Harmony Borax Works
Interpretive Trail

Devil's Hole
(Death Valley N.P.)

136

PANAMINT

Emigrant

190

Owens
Lake

Panamint
Dunes

Skidoo

Furnace Creek
Visitor Center &
Death Valley Museum

Death Valley

Zabriskie Point

395

Father Crowley
Point

EMIGRANT

Aguereberry
Point

Pyramid Peak
+ 6,703

190

Panamint
Springs

CANYON

Towne
Pass
4,956

Artists
Palette

BADWATER

127

Darwin
Falls

RD.

Wildrose Peak
9,064 +

Devils
Golf Course

Natural
Bridge

Death Valley
Junction

Olancha

Darwin

Charcoal
Kilns

190

GREENWATER RANGE

CHINA LAKE
NAVAL WEAPONS
CENTER

PANAMINT VALLEY RD.

Telescope Peak
11,049 +

Badwater Basin
(Lowest Point in
U.S., -282 ft.)

Dantes
View

AMARGOSA

Haiwee
Res.

Panamint City
(ghost town)

RANGE

RANGE

Coso Junction

Ballarat
(ghost town)

178

Shoshone

0   10   20 mi

0   10   20   30 km

Ashford Mill (ruins)

Salsberry Pass
3,315

127

395

N

This map of Death Valley National Park has red dots highlighting key cultural or tourist locations

Able to thrive even in drought conditions, tamarisks have added to Death Valley's greenness at the expense of other plants

services, and added more land to what had been the Death Valley National Monument. Covering 5,262 square miles (13,629 sq km), Death Valley is today the largest national park in the **contiguous** U.S. The park is about three times longer north-to-south than it is wide and is angled along the California–Nevada border. More than 90 percent of the park and nearly all of the tourist facilities are contained within California. The park's northeastern boundary (toward Nevada) follows straight lines, while most of the other borders conform to the irregular contours of the land.

Like many other parks in America, Death Valley today faces challenges relating to nonnative plant species. The introduction of such plants to the valley actually goes back about a century. Among the most **invasive** species were two types of tamarisk plants originally from the Eastern Hemisphere. These shrublike plants, which slightly resemble evergreen trees, were deliberately brought to Death Valley as a means of controlling erosion, creating wind breaks, and providing shade. They were planted by early pioneers, the CCC, and even the NPS before anyone suspected there would be negative consequences. The problem the tamarisks pose in Death Valley is that they crowd out native plants and absorb large amounts of water from the limited wetlands. Also, the plants' leaves can contain high amounts of salt, so when they fall, they can make the soil less fertile for other plants.

One type of tamarisk in Death Valley is called the saltcedar, and it produces countless fuzzy seeds that are carried on the wind throughout the region, further threatening native plants and the **ecosystem** as a whole. In 1972, government workers began removing tamarisk plants in various parts of Death Valley—efforts that continue today. Other nonnative species such as date and fan palms are also being eliminated, and the replanting of native shrubs and grasses is underway in hopes

of returning Death Valley's vegetation to its original state.

Death Valley today also faces air-quality issues—a problem that is the result not of actions within the park but of human activity to the west. Just as weather systems tend to travel west to east, so does air pollution. In the summer, the air tends to come from the southwest, which means emissions from power plants and vehicles in the sprawling Los Angeles metropolitan area drift toward Death Valley. These emissions eventually form sulfates and nitrates, harmful compounds that reduce visibility in the atmosphere and contribute to **acid rain**. Reduced visibility detracts from sightseeing in the park, limiting not only how far visitors can see but also the full colors and contrast of the region. Acid rain can be harmful to plant life and increases land erosion. In the winter months, weather patterns come more from the northwest, and Death Valley's air quality significantly improves.

Los Angeles has the biggest freeway system of any American city, and its huge volume of car traffic contributes to polluted air

A Summer Getaway in January

In recent years, Death Valley has welcomed about 800,000 tourists annually. To many of Death Valley's visitors, the appeal of the park is its atypical tourist season. During the time of year that most national parks are snowy and cold, Death Valley's daily highs finally drop below 90 °F (32 °C). These more tolerable temperatures also correspond with the park's better periods of air quality and therefore better sightseeing. Spring is the busiest season of all in Death Valley. Aside from the comfortable weather and clean air, springtime offers visitors their best chance to see the desert environment in bloom.

Death Valley is valued mostly by people who appreciate nature for nature's sake, as it offers fewer recreational activities than most national parks. Fishing or boating activities are nonexistent, horseback riding services are very limited, and few rock climbers practice their craft in the park. The main activities and services available to guests revolve around sightseeing and learning about Death Valley's natural and cultural history.

Much of the year, travel in air-conditioned vehicles is the only sensible way to tour the park. Fortunately, nearly 1,000 miles (1,609 km) of roadways lead to many of Death Valley's most notable attractions. The Furnace Creek Visitor Center is something of a central hub, or starting point, in the park and features ranger-staffed information services, a bookstore, and a small nearby museum detailing Death Valley's history of borax mining.

Cacti, such as the beavertail cactus (a kind of prickly pear cactus), can be seen in Death Valley National Park any time of year

From Furnace Creek, guests can travel north to points of interest that include the old Harmony Borax Works site, the ghost town of Rhyolite, Scotty's Castle, and Ubehebe Crater. The Harmony Borax Works site features wagons from the famed 20-mule teams along with the remains of old buildings. Rhyolite is located a few miles outside the park and has more standing ruins than any of the region's many ghost towns. The historic Scotty's Castle is an impressive sight and a time capsule of what Western luxury looked like in the 1920s and '30s. Tours through the mansion and the surrounding grounds fill up fast, so reservations are recommended. Ubehebe Crater is a large and well-defined volcanic crater about a half-mile (805 m) wide and 600 feet (183 m) deep.

Roads heading south from Furnace Creek Visitor Center lead to Artist's Palette, Devil's Golf Course, Badwater Basin, Zabriskie Point, and Dante's View. Artist's Palette is a rugged, sloping wall of volcanic rock that exhibits hues of red, pink, yellow, green, and purple, thanks to the presence of various minerals. Devil's Golf Course is not a grassy sports setting at all but rather a lumpy salt flat featuring large, irregular crystal formations that would make for nightmarish golf hazards. Badwater Basin features the lowest point in North America and is located near one of Death Valley's largest salt flats. Zabriskie Point and Dante's View offer some of the best panoramic views in the park. Gazing westward from these elevated locations, visitors can look across

From left to right, sightseeing hotspots: Artist's Palette, Devil's Golf Course, Badwater Basin, Dante's View, Zabriskie Point

salt flats and canyons framed by the Panamint Mountains—sights that are particularly remarkable at sunset and sunrise.

Traveling west from Furnace Creek, visitors reach Stovepipe Wells, Father Crowley Point, and the Wildrose charcoal kilns. Stovepipe Wells is a way station located near the Mesquite Flat sand dunes that offers conveniences such as a gas station, general store, gift shop, restaurant, hotel, and ranger office. Father Crowley Point is just west of another park village, Panamint Springs, and offers an overlook of ancient lava flows and Rainbow Canyon. The Wildrose charcoal kilns are 25-foot (8 m), beehive-shaped stone structures that were once used for turning wood into charcoal, a fuel that was used to refine the region's mineral ores in the late 1800s.

Evidence suggests the 10 Wildrose charcoal kilns (completed in 1877) were used for only 2 years, and they remain in good condition

Apart from Death Valley's primary roadways, various side roads lead to less frequented canyons, playas, and overlooks. However, some of these dirt or gravel paths require vehicles designed for off-road use. With the exception of service roads, all roadways are open to bicycles, and mountain bikes are a popular means of tackling routes that may be too rough for cars. Bicyclists must stay on the park's roads, however, and riding on hiking trails or peddling cross-country in wilderness areas is prohibited.

That leaves hiking as the remaining option for touring the park, and in terms of pure exploration, there's no better way to experience Death Valley than on foot. Park visitors who are willing to walk a couple miles off the roadways can enjoy such attractions as the Salt Creek Interpretive Trail, where spring-fed pools containing **endemic** pupfish can be seen. Short strolls will also take tourists to Golden Canyon and Natural Bridge. Golden Canyon's name comes from its glowing reflection

Hiking is the most common means of getting into the heart of Death Valley's landforms, but bikers are very welcome in the park

From left to right, some of Death Valley's most striking rock forms: Golden Canyon, Natural Bridge, Mosaic Canyon

at sunset, and Natural Bridge takes its name from the thick stone arch spanning a narrow canyon. Another popular, short jaunt winds through Mosaic Canyon, which features smooth marble walls of black, gray, and white.

Among the park's longest hikes is the Telescope Peak Trail, a strenuous, 14-mile (23 km) round trip that leads to the highest point in Death Valley. This and other mapped trails have their appeal, but what makes Death Valley such an alluring hiking destination is the fact that trails aren't really necessary. The park's desolate landscape makes most of the terrain suitable for walking, and, because of the wide-open visibility, the chances of becoming lost are low. Determined hikers can trek to just about any location they see by almost any path they choose. Only a few places throughout the park, such as sites near abandoned mines, are closed to hikers.

Backcountry campers are bound by a few more regulations, but they, too, have most of the park available to them,

While it may be difficult to get lost amid Death Valley's wide-open spaces, hikers must take precautions against the heat

From left to right, snapshots of the park: backcountry hiking, a horned lizard, Furnace Creek Inn, Stovepipe Wells way station

and backcountry campsites are not limited to specific locations, as is the case in many other national parks. As a general rule, backcountry campers must set up away from roads, developed areas of the park, and water sources that are important to the desert wildlife. Campfires are not permitted in the park's backcountry. Backcountry hiking and camping also may provide the best wildlife viewing opportunities in Death Valley. Guests interested in glimpsing snakes and lizards can do well at lower elevations, while those hoping to catch sight of mule deer or rare bighorn sheep are advised to seek higher altitudes.

Aside from backcountry camping, tourists can stay at one of Death Valley's 10 drive-in campgrounds or 4 lodging facilities. Most campgrounds accommodate both RVs and tents, though only Stovepipe Wells and Panamint Springs campgrounds offer RV hookups. Campgrounds at the park's highest and lowest elevations close for part of the year to protect campers from Death Valley's most extreme summer or winter weather. Shower services are available near only some campgrounds, and laundry facilities are found by only Furnace Creek. Because the park is rarely packed with visitors, only Furnace Creek campground accepts reservations.

Indoor lodging options in the park include Furnace Creek Inn, Furnace Creek Ranch, Panamint Springs Resort, and Stovepipe Wells Village. The historic Furnace Creek Inn rivals Scotty's Castle as the most impressive structure in Death Valley and features Spanish mission architecture, a spring-fed swimming pool, and rows of lush palm trees.

It also contains a fine restaurant and has tennis courts and a golf course nearby. Furnace Creek Ranch shares many of these recreational facilities but has simpler cabins or hotel-style rooms. Panamint Springs Resort is more rustic and lacks many of Furnace Creek's luxuries, but it does feature a restaurant with a typical American food menu. Stovepipe Wells Village is the most basic of all but has a small swimming pool for guests looking to beat the desert heat.

Man-made oases such as Furnace Creek Inn stand in sharp contrast to the harsh surrounding landscape, giving even greater emphasis to the extremes of Death Valley. And while there is some luxury to be found in the park, it is the desert environment and climatic challenges that call to Death Valley's visitors—visitors who take comfort in knowing that unbridled nature still has a place in America.

Death Valley is home to a population of mountain lions, but it is rare to catch sight of these reclusive big cats

The Ultimate Survivor

Coyotes seem adaptable to almost any climate and habitat in North America, from Alaska's uppermost reaches to Death Valley's sweltering deserts. Death Valley coyotes are most active during the night when they hunt—usually alone—for rabbits, rodents, and occasionally young deer, and they are capable of sprinting up to 40 miles (64 km) per hour when chasing prey. Coyotes are similar to some wolves in appearance and color, but they are noticeably smaller, rarely growing heavier than 30 pounds (14 kg) in hot climates. A coyote's distinctive howl is used to locate family or pack members or to warn rival coyotes away from a territory.

Defensive Desert Lizards

Southern Desert horned lizards are odd little reptiles found in deserts of the American Southwest. Their drab coloration and squat bodies resemble those of toads, and spikes grow from the backs of their heads and the sides of their bodies and short tails—traits that explain why the lizards are sometimes called horned toads. They are typically three to five inches (8–13 cm) long and primarily eat ants that they catch with extendable tongues. For defense, horned lizards usually rely on their

excellent camouflage or burrow into loose sand, but they are also surprisingly fast sprinters. To make themselves less appealing to predators, they also may puff up their bodies, hiss, bite, and— most disturbingly—even shoot blood from their eyes.

A Hidden Oasis

Tourists who want a change of pace from Death Valley's typical arid landscapes should consider the Darwin Falls Trail. This two-mile-long (3.2 km) hiking trail begins just west of Panamint Springs. It initially looks similar to other locations in the park, but as the trail winds farther into a small valley, the soil shows signs of moisture, and then a small stream emerges along the path. At the same time, vegetation transitions from dry shrubs to tall trees such as willows and cottonwoods. At the trail's end is Darwin Falls, an 80-foot (24 m) waterfall. Ferns surround the pool below, and songbirds chirp overhead, creating a unique Death Valley experience.

Gower Gulch Loop

Hikers wanting to get in the midst of Death Valley's desert landscapes near Furnace Creek often choose the Gower Gulch Loop. This moderately strenuous, four-mile (6.4 km) hiking trail begins in the colorful Golden

Canyon. Much of the trail was once a paved road that was destroyed by flash floods decades ago. Today, the dry washes that make up the trail weave through boulders and past old mines and rock formations such as Manly Beacon and Red Cathedral. Throughout the loop, many side paths are available for exploration, including a trail leading to the scenic overlook Zabriskie Point. Morning is typically the most comfortable and scenic time for this hike.

Three Hours to Another World

All the rain that doesn't fall in Death Valley has to fall somewhere. That somewhere is typically on the opposite side of the Sierra Nevada range, and driving about three hours westward from Death Valley to Sequoia National Forest can demonstrate the true impact of rain shadows.

This lush forest seems the total opposite of Death Valley and contains groves of some of the planet's largest and oldest trees; rivers and lakes suitable for whitewater rafting, kayaking, and fishing; and winter snowfalls perfect for cross-country skiing and snowshoeing. Sequoia National Forest also features hiking trails, rock climbing, cave tours, picnic areas, and camping.

The Same but Different

Death Valley visitors wanting a little twist on the desert experience can drive a couple hours southeast to the Mojave National Preserve. Like

Death Valley, this region features mountains, canyons, dry lakebeds, and fascinating rock formations. Plant and animal life is also similar, but there are a few differences that may make Mojave worth the trip. Its typical elevations are higher than Death Valley's, and it tends to be slightly cooler on average. The Mojave Preserve is less developed and receives fewer tourists, offering a more timeless feel. Mojave also permits hunting of wild game such as quail and mule deer.

Beating the Heat

Extreme heat is an obvious concern in Death Valley, especially in the summer, when thermometers often register above 120 °F (49 °C). The most obvious precaution is to visit the park during the cooler seasons. Those visitors willing to face the challenges of summer should keep large supplies of water handy, even if they plan to stay in air-conditioned vehicles, as automobiles commonly overheat and stall in Death Valley. Because of this potential for car problems, summer visitors may want to stick to only popular, paved roads in case assistance is needed from park rangers or other motorists. Attempting to walk for help in searing temperatures can be a fatal decision.

Creepy Creatures

Death Valley is home to predators such as mountain lions and coyotes, and while these animals can be dangerous, smaller creatures such as rattlesnakes, scorpions, and black widow spiders probably pose a greater risk to park visitors. These venomous and often hard-to-spot animals don't go out of their way to harm people but will defend themselves, so hikers should always be aware of where they're putting their hands and

feet. Hiking in groups is strongly advised in Death Valley. Cell phones may not get a signal in the park, and having an extra person available to seek assistance from ranger stations or park villages can mean faster medical attention in the event of receiving a poisonous bite or sting.

Glossary

acid rain: rain that is acidic, formed when emissions from burned fossil fuels combine with moisture in the atmosphere

adobe: a kind of clay that hardens when dried by the sun and is used to build structures

arid: lacking enough water for things to grow; dry and barren

backcountry: an area that is away from developed or populated areas

boom towns: towns that spring up or expand rapidly as a result of a surge, or "boom," in the local economy

claims: areas of land staked out by miners or homesteaders

contiguous: in physical contact; in the United States, contiguous states are all those except Alaska and Hawaii

ecosystem: a community of animals, plants, and other living things interacting together within an environment

endemic: native and limited to a particular country or region

eroded: worn away by the action of natural forces such as water, wind, or ice

faults: prominent breaks in the rock layers that make up Earth's crust; shifts or fractures may happen there, causing earthquakes or the growth of mountains

ice ages: periods in Earth's history when temperatures were much colder and glaciers covered much of the planet

invasive: (of plants) tending to spread harmfully, overtaking native species

talc: a soft, light-colored mineral with a greasy feel; it is used in making talcum powder and lubricants

washes: the dry beds of streams that flow only occasionally, usually in a ravine or canyon

Selected Bibliography

Christensen, Shane, et al. *National Parks of the American West*. New York: Wiley Publishing, 2010.

Gildart, Bert, and Jane Gildart. *Death Valley National Park*. Guilford, Conn.: The Globe Pequot Press, 2005.

Hirschmann, Fred, Randi Hirschmann, and Mark A. Schlenz. *Death Valley National Park*. Bozeman, Mont.: Companion Press, 1999.

National Geographic Guide to the National Parks of the United States. Washington, D.C.: National Geographic Society, 2009.

Palazzo, Robert P. *Death Valley*. Mount Pleasant, S.C.: Arcadia, 2008.

Schullery, Paul. *America's National Parks: The Spectacular Forces That Shaped Our Treasured Lands*. New York: DK Publishing, 2001.

White, Mel. *Complete National Parks of the United States*. Washington, D.C.: National Geographic Society, 2009.

Websites

Death Valley National Park
http://www.nps.gov/deva/index.htm
The official National Park Service site for Death Valley is the most complete online source for information on the park and includes a virtual museum.

National Geographic: Death Valley National Park
http://travel.nationalgeographic.com/travel/national-parks/death-valley-national-park/
This site provides a concise visitor's guide to Death Valley, complete with maps, photos, sightseeing suggestions, and links to other popular national parks.

Index

Death Valley
National Park

DATE DUE   56049
